Animal Look-Alikes
Alligators and Crocodiles

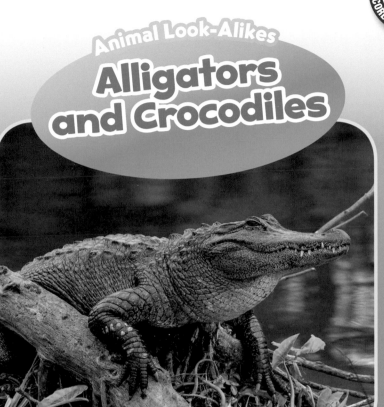

Joanne Mattern

RED
CHAIR
·PRESS·

Animal Look-Alikes is produced and published by Red Chair Press:

Red Chair Press LLC   PO Box 333   South Egremont, MA 01258-0333

www.redchairpress.com

About the Author

Joanne Mattern is the author of nearly 350 books for children and teens. She began writing when she was a little girl and just never stopped! Joanne loves nonfiction because she enjoys bringing science topics to life and showing young readers that nonfiction is full of compelling stories! Joanne lives in the Hudson Valley of New York State with her husband, four children, and several pets, which look nothing alike!

Publisher's Cataloging-In-Publication Data
Names: Mattern, Joanne, 1963-
Title: Alligators and crocodiles / Joanne Mattern.

Description: [South Egremont, Massachusetts] : Red Chair Press, [2018] | Series: Animal look-alikes | Interest age level: 006-010. | Includes science vocabulary, fun facts, and trivia about each type of animal. | "Core content library." | Includes bibliographical references. | Summary: "Long snout. Big teeth. Hard scales. Lives in warm climates. Is it an alligator or a crocodile? Look inside to learn how these beasts from the age of dinosaurs are alike and how they differ!"-- Provided by publisher.

Identifiers: LCCN 2016947288 | ISBN 978-1-63440-209-5 (library hardcover) | ISBN 978-1-63440-214-9 (ebook)

Subjects: LCSH: Alligators--Juvenile literature. | Crocodiles--Juvenile literature. | CYAC: Alligators. | Crocodiles.

Classification: LCC QL666.C925 M38 2018 (print) | LCC QL666.C925 (ebook) | DDC 597.98--dc23

Illustrations by Tim Haggerty.

Map illustration by Joe LeMonnier.

Photo credits: Shutterstock.

Printed in Canada

102017 1P FRNS18

Table of Contents

Alligator or Crocodile?

These two animals look a lot alike. And they do have a lot in common. But they are not the same! One of these animals is an alligator. The other is a crocodile. Although they have many things in common, there are ways to tell which is which. Let's learn the secrets of alligators and crocodiles!

?

Big Reptiles

Alligators and crocodiles are both members of the reptile family. Reptiles have some interesting features. Reptiles are cold-blooded. This means that they cannot control their body temperature. If a reptile is in a warm place, its body temperature goes up. If it is in a cold place, its body temperature goes down. To keep their body at the right temperature, reptiles often lie in the sun to warm up. If they get too hot, they dig a hole in the ground or take a swim in a pond to cool off.

Now You Know!

Other members of the reptile family are snakes, turtles, tortoises, lizards, and tuataras.

Reptiles are covered
in hard scales.

Reptiles have
backbones.

Reptiles may lie in
the sun to warm up.

Power Word: The word reptile
comes from 14th century Latin to
mean to creep or crawl.

Another thing reptiles have in common is their skin. Reptiles are covered with hard pieces of skin called scales. Reptiles also have a backbone and lungs to breathe air.

Some animals give birth to live babies, but not reptiles! Almost all reptiles lay eggs. Alligators and crocodiles lay between 35 and 70 eggs. Both animals dig a hole in the ground to make a nest. After the mother lays her eggs, she covers the eggs with dirt. Alligator eggs hatch in 65 days. Crocodiles take longer to hatch—about 80 days.

Scary Predators

Another thing alligators and crocodiles have in common is that they are both **predators**. Both of these animals eat meat. Crocodiles and alligators hunt for fish, frogs, birds, turtles, and raccoons. They may also eat large animals, like deer, wild pigs, and zebras. Once in a while, an alligator or a crocodile will attack a human. Watch out!

Both alligators and crocodiles are sneaky hunters. They lay quietly in the water. Only their nose, eyes, and ears stick out. These predators wait quietly until an animal comes too close. Then they jump up and grab the **prey**. Alligators and crocodiles do not take the time to chew their food. They just swallow it whole, or tear it into smaller pieces and gulp them down.

Now You Know!

The Nile crocodile will eat just about anything. But a bird called the Egyptian plover can walk right into the crocodile's mouth without getting hurt! The crocodile allows this because the plover cleans food from between the crocodile's teeth.

The Crocodile Family

Both alligators and crocodiles are part of a family called **crocodilians**. There are four different reptiles in the crocodilian family. The crocodilian family includes 14 species of crocodiles. Other crocodilians include two kinds of alligators, six kinds of caimans, and one gharial. Caimans look a lot like crocodiles, but they are a lot smaller. A gharial weighs up to 550 pounds (250 kg) and has a long, skinny **snout**.

Crocodilians are the world's biggest reptiles. The smallest crocodilian is named Cuvier's dwarf caiman. It's the size of a small adult. The largest is the Indopacific crocodile. This big guy can be more than 23 feet (7 m) long!

Now You Know!

Crocodilians are related to dinosaurs. But crocodilians lived on earth before dinosaurs did, and they survived after the dinosaurs died out.

These gharials are found in India.

In the Water

Both alligators and crocodiles spend a lot of time in the water. They are very strong swimmers. They use their webbed feet and long tail to move through the water. Alligators can only live in freshwater environments, such as ponds, **swamps**, ditches, lakes, and slow-moving rivers. Crocodiles can live in both freshwater and saltwater environments.

Alligators and crocodiles breathe through their nose when they are above the water. When they dive underwater, muscles close the nose holes so no water gets into the animal's lungs. Alligators and crocodiles also have a big flap of skin at the back of their mouths. This flap closes when the animal opens its mouth underwater to grab its prey.

Crocodiles and alligators can stay underwater for a long time. Their heart slows down and the blood vessels get smaller. These changes mean that the animal uses less oxygen. Crocodiles and alligators can stay underwater without breathing for more than an hour.

Now You Know!

Crocodiles can also jump! A crocodile may sometimes jump straight up in the air to catch a bird.

Running on Land

Crocodilians are great swimmers, and they can move very quickly on land too. These reptiles have three ways of moving on land. The first is the belly crawl. The animal pushes itself along the ground. The second way is the high walk. The crocodile or alligator stands up on its legs and runs about 9–10 miles per hour (15–16 km per hour).

The fastest way for an alligator or crocodile to move is the gallop. The animal uses its back legs to push the rest of its body forward in a kind of leap. Usually only smaller animals can do this, and they can only gallop over short distances. However, they can reach speeds of up to 20 miles (32 km) an hour.

Where in the World?

Alligators and crocodiles have a lot in common, but there are some easy ways to tell them apart. The biggest difference is where they live. Crocodiles live in a lot more places than alligators do. Crocodiles live in Africa, Asia, and parts of Australia, South America, and North America. Crocodiles only live where it is hot all year round. In North America, crocodiles live only in Mexico and southern Florida.

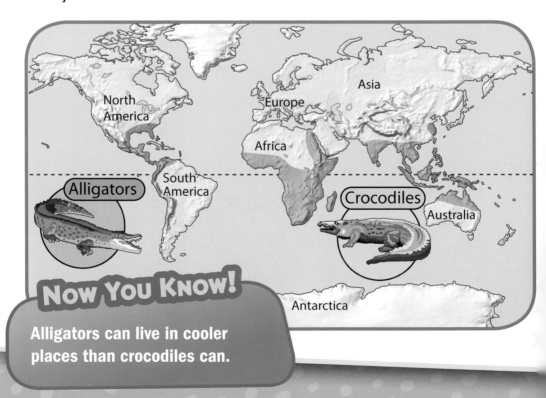

Now You Know!

Alligators can live in cooler places than crocodiles can.

Alligators only live in two places on earth. Almost all species of alligator live in North America. They live in Florida, Louisiana, and parts of Texas, Georgia, Alabama, North Carolina, and South Carolina. Another kind of alligator lives in a small area in China. This alligator is called the Chinese alligator. The Chinese alligator is much smaller than the American alligator. An American alligator can grow up to 15 feet (4.5 m) long, but a Chinese alligator is only about five feet (1.5 m) long.

Jaws and Teeth

Another way to tell alligators and crocodiles apart is by looking at their snout. An alligator's snout is round and shaped like the letter U. Its snout is bigger than a crocodile's snout. When an alligator closes its mouth, only its top teeth can be seen.

A crocodile's snout is long and narrow. It is shaped like the letter V. Also, when a crocodile closes its mouth, some of its top and bottom teeth stick out around the side of its snout. If you look closely at an American crocodile's snout, you can see a big tooth on either side of the lower jaw that fits into a slot in the upper jaw.

Now You Know!

When an alligator or a crocodile loses a tooth, another one grows in its place. A crocodilian can have thousands of teeth during its life!

rounded
snout
like a *U*

long and
narrow
like a *V*

All crocodilians have powerful muscles in their jaws. These muscles allow the animal to clamp its jaws shut so tightly that it is almost impossible to pull them apart. However, the muscles that open their jaws aren't very strong at all. For this reason, a person can tie a strip of cloth around an alligator or crocodile's jaws and the animal will not be able to open its mouth. A person might even be able to hold the animal's mouth shut with his or her bare hands!

An alligator or crocodile's jaws don't just chomp on prey. They also help these animals find food to eat. Both animals have thousands of tiny bumps on their jaws. These bumps can feel tiny movements in the water. These movements help the animal sense that a fish or another animal is near.

Scaly Colors

Another way to tell alligators and crocodiles apart is the color of their skin. Both of these animals are covered with thick, tough scales. These scales protect the animal from getting hurt. They also make the animal waterproof and protect it from the hot sun.

An alligator's scales are dark green or black. A crocodile's skin is gray or pale green and lighter in color than an alligator's scales. American crocodiles have dark stripes on their bodies and tails when they are babies, but these stripes fade away as the animal grows.

Both alligators and crocodiles use the color of their skin as **camouflage**. The colors blend in with the land around them and also help them hide in the water. This helps this fierce predator hide when it is waiting to catching its prey.

Power Word: The term camouflage was first used in World War I to describe tanks and buildings painted in disguise or to disappear.

Long Lives

Both alligators and crocodiles can live for a long time. Crocodiles live longer than alligators do. That is probably because they are larger. Crocodiles can live up to 70 years, and some may be more than 100 years old.

Alligators and caimans only live for 30 to 40 years. Animals that live in zoos or preserves usually live longer than animals in the wild. That is true because animals in a zoo have no natural predators and also have plenty of food to eat.

Now You Know!

Scientists can tell how old a crocodile or alligator is by looking at growth rings in the animals bones and teeth.

Keeping Alligators and Crocodiles Safe

Both alligators and crocodiles face **threats** from people. When people drain a swamp or build homes and businesses close to the water, alligators and crocodiles can lose their homes.

For many years, people killed these dangerous reptiles to protect themselves and their animals. Both animals were also hunted for their meat and their skin. Alligator and crocodile skin was used to make shoes, belts, purses, and more. By 1972, almost all crocodilians in the world were **endangered**.

Young alligator in Big Cypress National Preserve, Florida.

Since the 1970s, many countries have passed laws to protect alligators and crocodiles. The animals were given safe places to live. Crocodiles and alligators that threatened people were captured and moved to safer places. Luckily, all this work has paid off. Today, most of the populations of wild crocodiles and alligators are increasing.

King of the Reptiles

Alligators and crocodiles are not the same. Many things about their bodies and where they live are different. However, these animals also have many things in common. One of the most important things they share is their importance to the natural world. Alligators and crocodiles are important predators. They help keep nature in balance. And just like all other animals, alligators and crocodiles are special creatures. They may look a lot alike, but they are not the same! Each creature has its own special place on our planet.

Two-by-two. Crocodilians play an important role in nature's balance.

Glossary

camouflage coloring or markings on an animal's skin that help it blend in with its surroundings

crocodilians a family of reptiles that includes crocodiles, alligators, caimans, and gharials

endangered in danger of dying out

predators animals that hunt other animals for food

prey animals that are hunted by other animals for food

snout the nose and mouth of an animal

swamp an area of low-lying, wet ground

threat danger

Read More in the Library

Hirsch, Rebecca E. *American Alligators: Armored Roaring Reptiles.* Lerner, 2016.

Marsh, Laura. *Alligators and Crocodiles.* National Geographic Kids, 2015.